My Mind's Dark Parties

Khariis Ubiaro

My Mind's Dark Parties

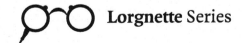 **Lorgnette** Series

First published in 2017
by Eyewear Publishing Ltd
Suite 333, 19-21 Crawford Street
Marylebone, London W1H 1PJ
United Kingdom

Typeset with graphic design by Edwin Smet
Author photograph by Elainea Emmott
Printed in England by Lightning Source

ISBN 978-1-911335-86-3

Eyewear wishes to thank Jonathan Wonham for his generous patronage of our press.

WWW.EYEWEARPUBLISHING.COM

'The road to hell
is paved with good intentions' –
My mum said this to me when I was 12.
I was so confused at the time. Thinking
'What does that have to do with anything'.
As I matured I understood. We all intend
to do great things but intention isn't
enough, talking and thinking about great
stuff doesn't get great stuff done. Action,
doing. Doing is how things get done. You
always wanted me to write mum, always
encouraging and believing in the words
that disperse from my mind. Thank you.
You are my drive, what keeps me
writing. This is for you.
The first of many.

For Mum.

TABLE OF CONTENTS

I'M STILL A MAN

12 *Years* proceeded and slavery still exists
a persistent pressure on my people so we dance for the whip
hop around get lean
society's fractured our hip
seduced by slave masters who caused us to slip
black
negative connotations from the day I was born
judged and looked at with caution before I was torn
out
ripped and snatched
straight from the womb
embraced by pure white hands
a cute baby baboon
me
our gold's gone and we race to win it back
he can't run
he can't rap
so instead he's selling some crack
drugs
his perspective
what he sees others doing
stereotypes get worse
negativity keeps brewing
why?
statistically stupid
most are without a father
financially deprived
times are only getting harder
land
lands taken
engulfed by foreign words
culture's now diluted; native tongues can't be heard

because we're ecstatic to be shackled
herded up in prisons
it's like negroes become cattle
whipped like horses being sat on with no saddle
here
play the maracas but we don't want to hear them rattle
you're not as academic
or even have an education
we'll reinvent you
recreate you
so stick to recreation
constipated; mothers constipated for nine months
releasing dirty struggles for officers to go on a hunt
don't –
SHOOT

Africa, ruled out as a country
infiltrated, sold so cheaply
find us on Gumtree
sat on unstable walls, had many falls, no Humpty Dumpty
dark honeycomb toffee sugar –
a racist meal
I become Crunchie chocolate
black
dark
opaque
midnight
Nubian citizen but I still see the light
so let me lay it down now and make it clear
I am a Kushite
I'm still a man

THIS IS MY BLOOD

poetry like poison
my hands shake words translate into toxins through my bloodstream
reaching my fingertips my blood spills into the format of words, my paper
my paper it needs to be cleansed
these are more than words, this is my blood translated
I thought my blood was red
instead my blood bleeds and reads
letters
sentences
there is a format to my blood
text and punctuation; punctured pores pouring my heart out

will you read my blood?

BROKEN BEAUTY

bewildered and brutally banished from beauty
she thinks she's
ugly
litter lit her emotions
she thinks she's trash
ignited by negative words
I want to extinguish her pain
but I can't, I can't, I can't do it
because I'm no hero
past relations have become her current affairs
she finds it hard to accept
cheated on the truth
she believes the lies
now bees leave the hive she's lost her home
lost her sense of belonging yet always longing to get it back
her exes have put an x on my chances of getting with her
she's branded by them
scorched and burned from the way she was treated am I defeated before a
        relationship has even commenced?
sun moon dark light black white yes no
you said I was both the good and bad in your life
your everything
but now you seem to have given up everything for fear of being hurt again
adopting xenophobia as your child for fear of not knowing what's to come we're
finally done before we've even begun
I would have taken my chances
trust
trust was used as a blade and thrust through your heart
broken like eggshells on a constant except your yoke was pain
I tried to convey a cause clarity that my kisses could become the remedy to
        your bruised lips but

you'd rather be a lone wolf because
love to you is about as rare as a lunar eclipse
you once told me to look deep into your eyes and challenge the concept of
    anyone caring about me more than you do
but you regressed
regressed into that little girl who was once oppressed and depressed over
    the fact that
she could never get anything off of her chest
you regressed
you
regressed

LOVE TO THE POWER OF ONE

my ignorance and lack of love gently placed her heart into a blender
I watched as my attitude wrestled with her emotions
I couldn't love myself enough to see why I should be loved
I took what could have been unconditional for granted
pocketing it for rainy days
but hear what I say
how dare you love me before I do

WHO'S REALLY IN CHARGE HERE?

I saw a glitch in the life of all else
maybe the gods look down on our infamous vulnerabilities that succumb
       to systems of disbelief in ourselves
I think that Adam and Eve were adamant to leave the garden of Eden
substituted eternal life for knowledge and bleeding
and with that the dire knowledge that we die and become subject to death
demoted from the degree of immortality earned
I've learned that being human is being at the centre of the universe
watching life revolve and unfold around you
being human is staying loyal and rooted to the earth that you are bound to
1 2 3
I'm one to be free for the rest of my life
there's something about humanity
we are the apples on our own trees, forgetting that we are also
the roots
but still
we aspire to be godlike
desperate for state-of-the-art fittings
yet still desperate to fit in and aspire to be like those we place on pedestals
I've watched petals fall
are you aware that flowers kill one another?
nature's reversed and babies kill mothers
hate the despised lovers

who's really in charge here?
who's really in charge here?
how much do you charge here?
'cause I can't find my charger

maybe Zeus the father should supply the villages with electricity instead
I said Zeus because he's basically my friend

15

part the Red Sea like Moses because Poseidon taught me how to water bend
yet I'll watch the young die of thirst and be the first to say that I haven't got
    a penny to lend
maybe we'll meet Hades in the end if we continue to follow our flesh
I wish my words could express how apologetic I am
Apollo didn't get it because he's more than a man
so I say have it Yahweh and not your way
yet mankind believes God is the one to make mistakes
I have proof
solid proof
it's here down to a prophetic precision
mankind aspires to be godlike based on one foolish decision
because God created man but man created religion

HUMANOVA

cosmic radiation took its toll
seeping its energy into our planet
planting his seed for Mother Earth to breed
his children
children of the light from galaxies beyond
no they don't belong here
but are here
hear how they are here to entertain and inspire us
while they sit on thrones saying to the general public
we applaud you because you admire us
signing autographs here and there might tire
but we appeal to the cold industry of fans so our managers can't fire
since when did stars begin to be managed and controlled
used as pawns in a game of chess yet still he wants to be king so he's called
       a rogue
one size up and she can't be a *Vogue*
model
because in some shape or form we're all supernovas and feel like taking off
yet to make it and get somewhere at great cost
at great loss and requires a great boss
or does it? she asks
size, age, name
it shouldn't matter
red dwarf, blue giant
both stars made of matter
different planets, still gods
Venus, Neptune and Mars
so it's possible
possible that those beams and flashes of light walk amongst us from day to day
I wear Orion's belt and eat Milky Way
bars

even the Son has a father
so what's out there is down here
Corona in my bloodstream over lager
stars are born within us
we're made up of the same energy
same entity
sharing the same common enemy
stars aren't meant to be dimmed, dictated or controlled
let's shine our lights freely and continue to explode
let me introduce you to strobe
lights
our mutual friend
mutual friend who shares the same goal
we made a decree to cause darkness to flee
as darkness sees our face he cries
woe is me
moonlit beings walk the earth
shining their lights
supplements to the dirt
normality is hurt
we stole his chance to be different
creating SETI to flirt
with beings that are better than us
every time a star dies a child is born
every time a child dies a star respawns
the cycle of life
a dark night so we are mourning, in the morning they say joy comes
nebula
the space from which stars were created
formed from piles of dust and breath as we were
so I agree
not all stars are born in space
some walk among us within the human race

LONE WOLF

forgotten like the rotten apple that solemnly sits seedless –
secluded in the corner
liberated from a nostalgic pack
he made a pact to prevail alone
an ominous outsider who outlived the oppressor
impressed by his inability to become infatuated by another
movements like dance
deviating from the rhythm of a normal man
predator that prays for moral peace

I am a
lone wolf

THE NOISE IN MY HEAD

I just need to quiet the noise in my head
the noise that doesn't belong to a particular voice, the noise of insanity, I dread
I dread, I dread, I dread what's being said
influenced and infiltrated, engulfed and emancipated
the noise in my head has taken over
a cacophony of sounds, an anthem in the round, screams, sirens, pure vulgarity
 and violence, I can't deal
the noise in my head disabled my ability to feel
to feel and thrive but caused a lack of emotion
a crowd of consequences from noises within my head
this noise tells me that I'm better off dead better off sitting in a gutter, flickers
 and flutters
onomatopoeia I need it to stop
headed in and hearing from the wrong direction
an ultimate inception
I just need to quiet the noise in my head

MY MIND'S DARK PARTY

there is beauty in death
changing states, passing though this life into the next
souls changing, passing through liberal matter

IMAGINATION IS AN EYE

imagination is an eye within itself
positive thoughts and ideas sustain good mental health

realms that manifest pigments from extraterrestrial entities dissected fractions
        and segments from another plane influencing the way we live,
        a poisoned potential
– one that doubts surrealism
it is disbelief that creates a corrosive heart
imagine, imagining is the key to seeing externally what we as people
        internally desire
synergy between thoughts to summon our ambition
our hope
our freedom
freedom to dwell within another dimension
not to mention that we are products of our own making
induced with digested doctrines
yes
but we have a choice
a choice to listen to that subtle subconscious voice that speaks
speaks to no-one but ourselves
to create ideas that become viral and spread like disease, a rapid growth
        of franchise and branches, to create paper from trees
the origins of all came from one mind
to share thoughts and feelings and plans and meaning
from mind to mind
but I don't mind sounding peculiar and abnormal
realise and recognise that everything happens first inside
so know that thoughts create paths that steadily create literal roads
playing with paper planes in plain sight, a stimulus to build and unfold
the highest form of creativity through thought is imagination
imagine a nation of people that thought and fought for themselves,
        emancipated from mental slavery

it is no-one but ourselves that can free our minds

cascading cans of cans and can'ts creep into calm minds
can'ts corrupt and cans congratulate
conflict is caused between the clauses
the collateral damage is us
convicted by crude conversations that congregate in our minds
so-called coincidental casualties conspired with our beings
castrating crystal clear thoughts
these are the thoughts of others that try to influence our own

imagination is an eye within itself
positive thoughts and ideas sustain good mental health

they never let her pour the thoughts that flowed like water out of her mind
Jew, Gentile, other, mankind,
still one people, still a nation,
but I write to ask for premature cremation –
death by fire but unlike the phoenix we will not be rising from the ashes
persecuted and yet we are the ethnic majority
if roses are red, why call violets blue?
it's like we welcome imposed ideas and let what's false become true
we're being controlled and looked down on every hour
a higher power believing they're the sons of light, I call them sunflowers
a defiled promise that we'd have a better quality of life
enslaved to the so-called Aryan 24/7, 9-5
there's a huge difference between living and being alive
we're in a maze with few exits, I don't even believe there's a map
see they proclaim to be flowers, I agree
but more like Venus flytraps
the one thing we all yearn for is an immaculate quick death
I watched families turn to faeces and fathers neglect their baby's breath
it's like I'm in a realm of distortion
murder's most certainly okay as is an immediate abortion
and if abortion isn't an option you could always be an orphan or a crushed
orchid
there's a mental struggle to place yourself above another being, now that's
real contortion
we thought the wars ended after the first
but here's the thing about wars
wars will never end if we use weapons to fight
love conquers all, love will win wars
and all is fair in love and war
but they love a war
and any love that once took residence in my heart has now converted into

hate
I hate them
despise them
detest them
what they have done to us is unforgivable

Lightning Source UK Ltd.
Milton Keynes UK
UKOW01f0306311017
311921UK00001B/56/P